S0-ART-606

HURRAY FOR B.C.

Selected Cartoons from
THE SUNDAY BEST OF B.C.

BY JOHNNY HART

Foreword by Bill Mauldin

A FAWCETT GOLD MEDAL BOOK

Fawcett Publications, Inc., Greenwich, Conn.
Member of American Book Publishers Council, Inc.

To Curls, Jack, Peter, Thornton and Wiley.

YOU KNOW WHO YOU ARE.

my thanks,

Johnny Hart

Library of Congress Catalog Card Number: 64-10402

Manufactured in the United States of America

FOREWORD

B.C. is one of the most brilliant examples of what is generally considered, by Johnny Hart's younger fans, as the "new school" of comic strips. Actually, as his older fans know (and there are more of them than he might think), it is in a grand old tradition which goes all the way back to 1911 and the beginning of *Krazy Kat.* Or, if you want more recent examples, there are *Toonerville Folks* (1924), *Barnaby* (1942), and *Sad Sack,* of World War II vintage.

All of these strips had two things in common: they were extremely, deeply funny, and they appeared to have been drawn in great haste. It was generally assumed by their devoted readers that their creators were so exhausted by the time they had thought up the ideas that they had nothing left to put into the art work.

Not so. The easiest picture in the world to draw is a cluttered one. Comic artists who fill every square inch with detail are known as "rivet men" in the trade, from the fact that they put every rivet on every boiler. What does it matter if the hero is a little offside in the panel? Stick in a computing machine, with hundreds of dials, or a tree, with every leaf. Nothing dazzles the customers like drawing every leaf on a tree.

But place two unwashed cavemen against a horizontal line, which could be the top of a swamp or the bottom of an overcast, or against a sloping line which could be the side of a hill or the edge of a rainbow, and you'd better place them right.

Not that Johnny Hart neglects truly important details in his work. What comic artist ever before took the trouble to research the exact sound of a lightning bolt striking? Thanks to Hart, the world knows today that it is "ZOT!" The artist will never be the same, but mankind is richer for the knowledge. And there are probably fewer than 10,000 serious paleantologists on the entire face of the globe who don't incline their heads respectfully at the mention of Hart's name, because he is the man who put "GRONK!" into a dinosaur's mouth. What else could a dinosaur say? Still, it took someone to first realize it.

There will be those who disagree with all I've said. The beginning term at every art school is crowded with kids who think that if you paint both eyes on one side of a nose you're on your way to being Picasso. And now there will be hordes of beady-eyed youngsters who will think that by free-wheeling drawing they can imitate Johnny Hart.

There might be a very few who can approach his draftsmanship, but there will never be another wit like his. Maybe it's just as well. Two such brains might constitute a critical mass, and then *B.C.* would have been responsible for a new kind of nuclear explosion, as well as the pre-Neanderthal discovery of fire, the wheel, sex, philosophy, and poetic whimsy.

BILL MAULDIN

Curls. A Master of sarcastic wit.

The Girls. (sigh)

Peter. A self-styled genius. The world's first philosophical failure.

B. C. a humble, meek, kind, naive slob. A pleasant encounter for those who don't like encounters.

Clumsy Carp, a friendly, unassuming maladroit. An assiduous student of ichtheology.

Wiley, a superstitious poet with an aversion to water in any form.

Thor. Inventor, artist, ladies' man. The inventor of the wheel, and the comb.

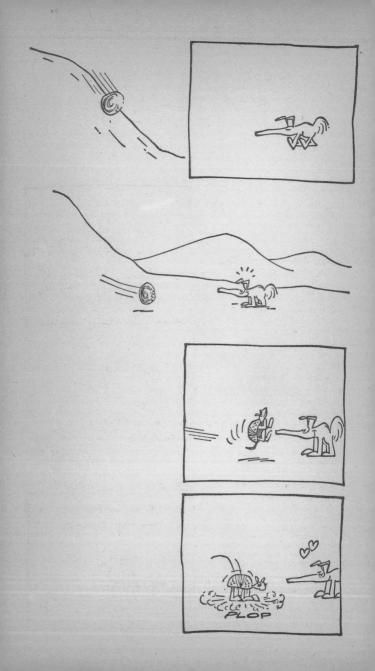

PLOP

ZIP

?

MAYBE I'VE GOT ANTBREATH.

IN PROVING TO YOU RATHER DENSE INDIVIDUALS THAT PARALLEL LINES NEVER MEET—

-- I AM ABOUT TO EMBARK UPON A HERETOFORE UNPRECEDENTED EXPEDITION WHICH WILL ENCOMPASS THE GLOBE.

SEE YOU.

FIFTY THOUSAND MILES LATER.

MY NEW RAFT-STEERING DEVICE

SAY -- THAT'S A REAL GAS, THOR.

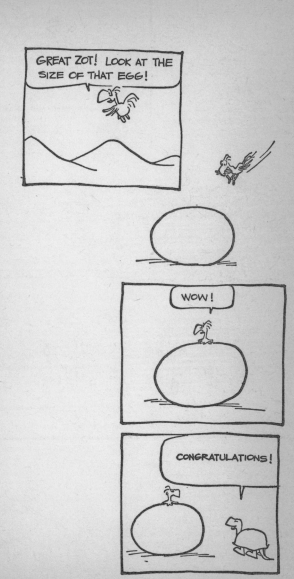

I WONDER WHERE YOUR SHADOW GOES WHEN YOU GO THROUGH A TUNNEL?

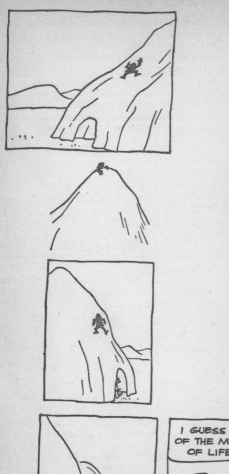

I GUESS IT'S JUST ONE OF THE MYSTERIES OF LIFE.

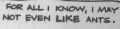

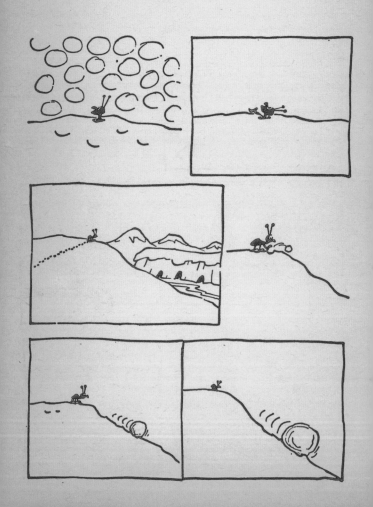

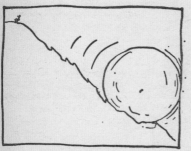

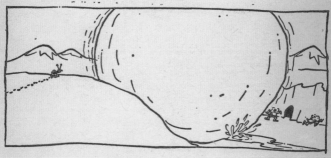

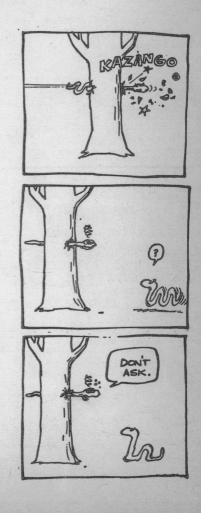

ten o'clock and all's well !

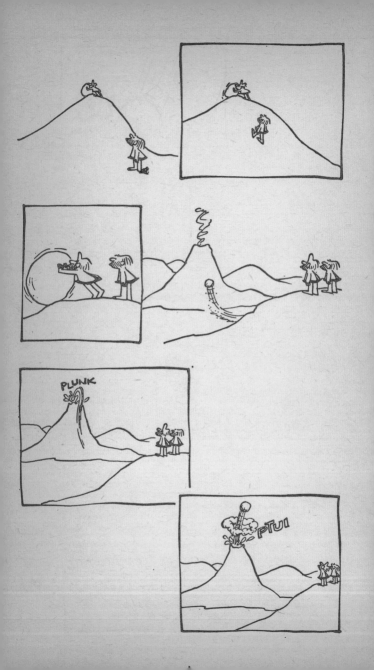

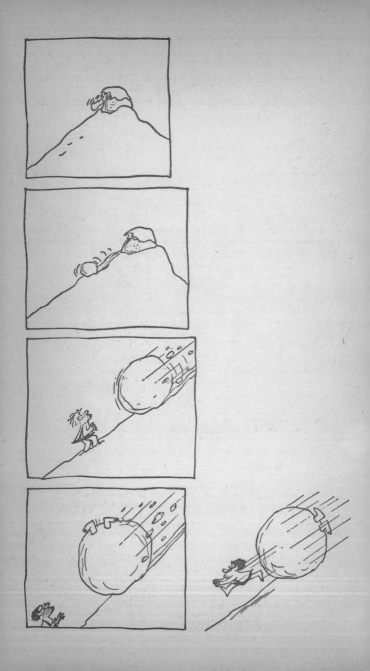

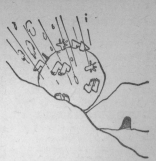

CHOP
CHOP
CHOP
CHOP

CHOP
CHOP
CHOP
CHOP
CHOP
CHOP

WE WERE REALLY LUCKY ON THAT ONE.

WHAT THE HECK IS THAT?

THIS IS A GOLF BAG, FOR MY MANY AND VARIOUS CLUBS.

THIS COMPARTMENT IS FOR THE MASHIE.

THAT'S FOR WHEN YOU GET MAD AT THE BALL, AND WANT TO MASH IT INTO THE GROUND.

THIS IS THE FLANGED NIBLIC.

THAT'S FOR IN CASE YOU RUN INTO A FEROCIOUS NIBLIC ON THE COURSE, YOU CAN FLANGE IT RIGHT IN THE MOUTH.

I'LL KICK OFF TO YOU!

RIGHT!

TOE GOT STUCK IN ONE OF THE LITTLE HOLES.

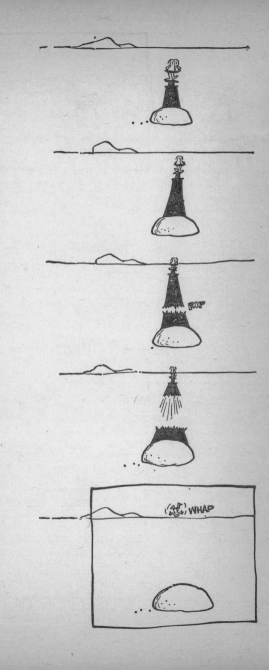

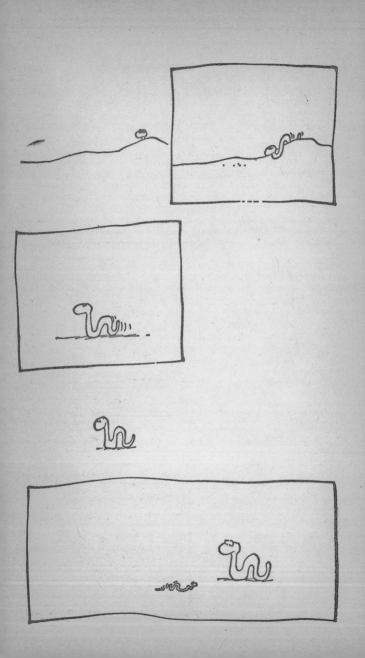

MAN, ANYBODY THAT DOESN'T LIKE HARD-BOILED EGGS IS SCREWY!

OOOO! MAYBE I'M SQUEEZING HIM TOO HARD!
GEE! I OUGHT TO PUT HIM BACK. I SHOULDN'T KEEP HIM HE'S THE LAST OF THE SPECIES!
WHANG

69-3-2